Fratelli Alinari

The Archives

Printing procedures in the Alinari Archives

The photographic files

The new photographic campaigns

The Art Printworks

The Publishing House

The Museum

The library

The instruments for photography

The image presented
and the image preserved

The photographic exhibitions

Graphic layout
Stefano Rovai - Graphiti

Photographs
George Tatge
Pierpaolo Pagano
Michele Burchi
Lorenzo Ceva

Printed in the month
of February 1993
by Grafiche Zanini
Bologna, Italy

Notes to the captions

Photographs published with the reference « **Alinari Archives** » are always *recent prints* (« contact » or « enlargements ») done in our photographic studio and taken from *original period negatives* (plates) or *original modern negatives* (film) owned by and preserved in the Fratelli Alinari Stabilimento. The pictures labeled « **Museo di Storia della fotografia Fratelli Alinari** » are always *original photographic prints* (vintage prints) owned by the Museum and kept there.

The term « **archives with the photographer's name** » (ex. Wulz archives) indicates a corpus of negatives and/or prints — often accompanied by cameras, documents, letters, advertising, etc. — which taken together, both in number and quality, document the activity of a photographer, a firm, an atelier.

The term « **family archives** » indicates a picture from a group of photographs constituting and bearing witness to the history of a family.

The indication « **fund** » refers to a group of over 25 vintage prints by the same photographer.

The entry « **collection** », in italics, like all references to the historical provenance of the picture, indicates a collection of prints and/or negatives put together by an expert in the subject according to various parameters, critical as well as historical.

If the photographic material or the object was acquired by the Museum or the Archives thanks to a « **donation** », the name of the donor is given in the caption. When the term « Alinari Archives » is preceded in the caption by the name of the Archives of a Corporation, an Enterprise, a public or private Institution, an Agency etc., it means that the material does not belong to Alinari, but is bound to Alinari by a contract of management.

The reference to the name of the photographer indicated after the entry « Alinari Archives » indicates that the picture was taken by a technical member of the Alinari staff, while if the name appears before this entry, it signifies that the picture was commissioned by Alinari Archives. In both cases, if it is an original print, signed and numbered by the photographer, the indication « Alinari Archives » is replaced by « Museo di Storia della fotografia Fratelli Alinari ».

Fratelli Alinari
Florence ''1852-1992''

Alinari's 140 years of history coincide in great part with the history of photography itself. Alinari: first and foremost a dynasty of photographers. But also, as the oldest firm in the world in the field of image making, an ever-present name in the day by day development of communication. Guardian of a patrimony of **1,500,000 historical photographs**, the archives of Italy's history, social fabric, art and culture. Of our collective memory. ■ **A**linari today is furthermore the heir — probably the sole heir — to those insuperable 19th-century artisan techniques employed in reproducing works of art in collotype printing and bringing the old glass plate negatives of our history back to life in contact prints and sepia toning. ■ **T**he Publishing House is a leader in the field of books on photography. In the past few years Alinari revived its photographic campaigns, recreating the Alinari style in a modern key. The firm is winning acclaim for its ability in finding photographs the world over, assembling images, producing books, exhibitions, multi-media shows, posters: creating in other words an « **image-integrated communication by images''**. ■ **A**linari is also a Museum — the only one in Italy and one of the few in the world in its field — custodian of a patrimony of over 150 historical and semiological photographic archives, basic

to the history of photography, ranging from the earliest daguerreotypes to today's holograms. ■ **T**hirty-five exhibitions in Florence in seven years. Another 45 in Italy and the rest of the world. The « Alicon » project: 400,000 plates; 750,000 negatives on film; 350,000 vintage prints which will become **15 million data-images** which can be called up in over 1,500 identification categories. The challenge is to make one of the greatest photographic archives in the world scientifically productive and economically profitable. **Alinari's contribution to the « Europe of images »**. ■ **M**usic and the image are the two great expressive means that permit communication beyond all barriers of language and of diversity. Elements of culture and aggregation that are not always easy to realize. We are attempting to take on and meet this ambitious challenge. ■ **T**his booklet intends to synthesize what Alinari is and what it will become.

Claudio de Polo
President - Director General
Fratelli Alinari

Fratelli Alinari, Royal estate of S. Rossore.
Holm-oak in the riding-track, circa 1915 (Alinari archives)

Fratelli Alinari

Fratelli Alinari, Self portrait of Giuseppe, Romualdo and Leopoldo Alinari, circa 1865 (Alinari archives)

Fratelli Alinari, founded in Florence in 1852, is the oldest firm in the world actively engaged in the field of photography, the world of images and communication. ■ Ever since 1863, the main headquarters have been in « Palazzo Alinari » in Via Nazionale 8 (now Largo Alinari 15), originally the site of the famous and highly popular photographic studio, but other prestigious premises are in the 15th-century Palazzo Rucellai, designed by L.B. Alberti. ■ The « historical » institutions, including the archives, the art printworks, the publishing house and the photographic files were joined by the Museo di Storia della fotografia Fratelli Alinari, inaugurated in 1985 in Palazzo Rucellai. The first of its kind in Italy and one of the sixteen to be found throughout the world, it is at present the only national institution dedicated exclusively to photographic exhibitions and has been host to about thirty-five exibition in its first seven years of activity. ■ As soon as it was founded, the Museum initiated an intense policy of new acquisitions and has received many highly important donations. The Alinari Archives

Fratelli Alinari, The Alinari Workshop:
the courtyard, the entrance on Via Nazionale 8
and a group of employees, early 1900s
(Alinari archives)

Fratelli Alinari, The terrace of the Alinari Workshop with the frames set
in the sun for contact printing, early 1900s (Alinari archives)

Fratelli Alinari, The Alinari Workshop:
washing the plates, early 1900s
(Alinari archives)

Fratelli Alinari, The Alinari Workshop:
portrait studio, early 1900s
(Alinari archives)

Fratelli Alinari, Waiting room of the Alinari Workshop,
early 1900 (Alinari archives)

Stabilimento Giacomo Brogi,
The King of Siam, 1897
(Alinari Archives - Brogi archives)

have once more begun their photographic campaigns, entrusted to famous professional photographers and coordinated by George Tatge. ■ The Florentine bookshop and the « Spazio Alinari per la fotografia » in Rome, which also has a bookshop, photographic files and exhibition space, complete the activities of the firm, reconfirming the historical presence of Alinari not only in Florence, but in Rome as well, where the first shop bearing the Florentine corporate symbol was opened in 1872, followed in subsequent decades by analogous points of reference in Naples, Venice and abroad. ■ Incomparable photographic archives (1,500,000 historical pictures in prints, vintage prints and negatives, 600,000 of which are in the Villani archives, recently acquired and kept in Bologna), an uninterrupted program of exhibitions and publishing activity, a broad acquisition strategy leading to the constant growth of the « image bank », soon transferred from the microfiches currently in use to supports such as the database and optical disks, are the characteristics that distinguish Fratelli Alinari, making the firm an international point of reference, a leader in the field, indispensable for photography and image communication.

Stabilimento Giacomo Brogi,
William II King of Prussia
(Alinari Archives - Brogi archives)

Stabilimento Giacomo Brogi,
Camillo Benso Count of Cavour
(Alinari Archives - Brogi archives)

Stabilimento Giacomo Brogi,
Queen Victoria
(Alinari Archives - Brogi archives)

F.P. Michetti, Gabriele D'Annunzio
(Alinari Archives - Michetti archives)

Fratelli Alinari, Giuseppe Garibaldi
(Alinari archives)

Fratelli Alinari, Victor Emmanuel II
(Alinari archives)

Fratelli Alinari, Florence. View of the Cathedral from Palazzo Vecchio, early 1900 (Alinari archives)

Fratelli Alinari, Carloforte, Island of S. Pietro. Sardinian costumes, early 1900s (Alinari archives)

Fratelli Alinari, Mont Blanc, early 1900s (Alinari archives)

The Archives

This is where the vast documentary heritage regarding customs, art, economy and the society in Italy and Europe from the second half of the 19th century to the present is safeguarded, thanks to the unceasing work of the famous Alinari atelier or photographic studio in the past century (shortly to be opened anew in updated form) and the ubiquitous photographic campaigns whose purpose was to document the history of Italy and Europe and to satisfy the demands of scholars and all those who might be interested, including the protagonists of the Grand Tour. ■ **A** discriminating policy of accessions and new photographic campaigns constantly integrate and diversify this heritage. Thanks to the enlightened work of acquisition and conservation on the part of Senator Cini, the « historical » collections of negatives on glass plates — Alinari, Anderson, Brogi, Chauffourier, Fiorentini and Mannelli — were expanded. ■ **T**he collections have recently been enlarged by other 19th and 20th century archives, some well-known, others less so (but just as important for the history of photography), on glass plates and on black/white and color film, such as Wulz, Michetti, Nunes Vais, Bombelli, Mollino, Betti-Borra, Zannier, Pozzar, Balocchi, Vannucci Zauli, Unterveger, Tuminello, Muzzani, Miniati, Morpurgo, Parma Borbone (to name only a few), and thanks to splendid private collections as well as generous donations. ■ **M**ention should be made above all of the acquisition of the entire Villani archives — the

Fratelli Alinari, Nicolosi. Mount Etna.
Monte del Filosofo and Montagnola,
early 1900s (Alinari archives)

Fratelli Alinari, Portotorres. Unloading
the tunny-fish, early 1900s
(Alinari archives)

G. Chauffourier, Naples. Drum vender, late 1800s (Alinari Archives - Chauffourier archives)

D. Anderson, Peasants of Ciociaria, late 1800
(Alinari Archives - Anderson archives)

equivalent of Alinari in 20th-century Bologna active from 1920 to 1980 and an indispensable link in forming, together with the Alinari Archives, a complete iconographic documentation that ranges from the middle of the 19th century up to the present. ■ The archives will remain in Bologna, where they are open to the public but will also be duplicated on microfiches and subsequently on video discs and data base, to facilitate consultation in Florence and elsewhere. ■ At present the Alinari Archives, to whom the safekeeping of some of the most important historical negatives in the world has been entrusted, include 400,000 glass plates and 750,000 negatives on film. They are therefore an inexhaustible font of images to be drawn on for use in exhibitions, books and television programs, didactic instruments and all types of publications, including advertising, and where private individuals as well as scholars (architects, historians, economists, semiologists) can find what they require.

P. Lazzaroni, Marina, circa 1905 (Alinari Archives - Lazzaroni family archives- *Lazzaroni donation*)

Fratelli Alinari, S. Rossore, circa 1865 (Alinari archives)

R. Pozzar, The ship 'Pia Costa' in the port of Monfalcone, circa 1957
(Alinari Archives - Pozzar archives)

Panatta, Rome. Statue of the colossus in the Palazzo dei Conservatori, circa 1940
(Alinari Archives - Panatta archives)

Bombelli, Brera Academy, Milan, circa 1930
(Alinari Archives - Bombelli archives)

Panatta, Rome.
View from the Dome
of St. Peter's,
circa 1930
(Alinari Archives
- Panatta archives)

A. Vallerini,
Pisa.
Lungarni
with the church
of Santa Maria
della Spina,
circa 1880
(Alinari Archives
- Vallerini
archives
- *Vallerini
donation*)

G. Wulz, Vittorio and Carlo Wulz during a game, circa 1890
(Alinari Archives - Wulz archives)

W. Wulz, I + cat, 1932 (Alinari Archives - Wulz archives)

36

V. Balocchi, Preparing her dowry, circa 1916
(Alinari Archives - Balocchi archives)

G. Vannucci Zauli, Female nude, circa 1940
(Alinari Archives - Vannucci Zauli archives - *Vannucci-Zauli donation*)

L. Betti, Still life, circa 1935
(Alinari Archives - Betti Borra archives)

**Alinari photographs in folders,
passe-partout or portfolios**

Printing techniques of the Alinari Archives

Fratelli Alinari, The Alinari Workshop: phases in printing, early 1900s (Alinari archives)

The printers in the Alinari darkrooms continue to print from the original glass plate negatives using methods and materials perhaps still used only by them. ■ Most of the prints requested are produced on bromographers, old contact printers, using the highest quality papers available on the market. ■ The prints can also be sepia toned, and in any case are each handled manually by the printer. ■ The pictures, printed for editorial use, for exhibitions, for commercial or decorative purposes, are either contact printed in the « classic » 21×27 cm format or enlarged up to mural-size. ■ The prints can be mounted in elegant passe-partouts, portfolio folders or framed for immediate hanging.

**Alinari photographic enlargements
for use in interior design**

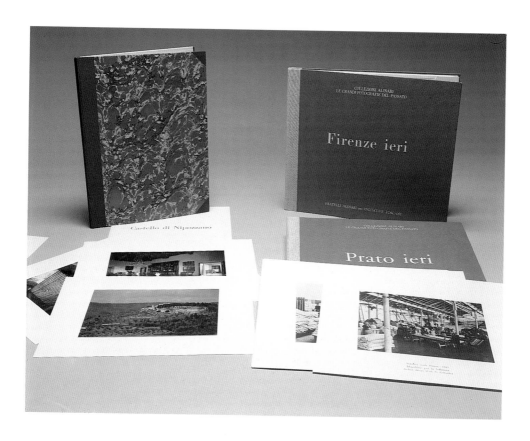

The photographic files

The photographic files in Florence and the photo collections in microfiches

Located in the prestigious Palazzo Rucellai, the Alinari photographic files justly lay claim to being one of the largest international centers of photographic documentation and are regularly visited by people from all over the world. Anyone who so desires may consult the files of the 300,000 black/white photographs in albums and the 200,000 images on microfiches from the « historical » collection, now also including the Wulz collection on data base and those in other archives and request photographic prints of almost any negative in the Archives. ■ More recently the photographic archives have also become exclusive agent in Italy for the most important photographic archives in Germany (Marburg) and in France (Giraudon). With 1,300,000 images on microfiches of artistic, historical, semiological subjects from the Marburg archives and a substantial selection of the 400,000 black/white photos and 60,000 ektachromes of Giraudon available for consultation and use. ■ The photographic files are also connected to the Villani archives in Bologna, and can therefore dispose of a further 650,000 pictures dealing with Italian industry, economy, history and society from 1920

I. Zannier, The coasts and mountains of Italy,
1967-1975 (Alinari Archives - Zannier archives)

P. Rivetti, Humming birds, circa 1970
(Alinari Archives - Rivetti archives -
C.ssa Rucellai donation)

up to date. ■ Since January 1991 the Alinari photographic files also handle the circa 20,000 color photographs of the large SEAT Divisione Stet Archives, which deal with lesser known examples of architecture, « hidden » museums and the unacknowledged artistic heritage scattered throughout Italy, and the circa 30,000 black/white and color photos of the Regione Umbria, referring to the industrial archaeology of the region, the Franciscan exhibitions, and the documentation of works of art in Umbria, including those by Raphael, Perugino, etc. The George Eastman House photographic collection in Rochester and the national French photographic files of St. Cir can also be consulted by scholars on video discs in the photographic files, exclusively for study purposes. ■ Upon request, the service staff of the files also undertake iconographic studies, both thematic and monographic, in other archives, collections, libraries, corporations and industries, national and international to track down the subjects in question.

Le paradis terrestre, fol. 25 v., Chantilly, Musée Condé
(Giraudon Archives - Alinari Archives)

A. Dürer, *Dürers Mutter*, Berlin, Staatliche Museen,
Kupferstichkabinett (Marburg Archives - Alinari Archives)

Simone Martini, Chapel of St. Martin, det., Assisi, Lower Church (Fototeca Ufficio Beni A.A.A.A.S. Regione dell'Umbria - Alinari Archives)

Altar-piece by Matteo di Giovanni, det., Montespertoli (Gr), Church of San Niccolò (SEAT Archives - Alinari Archives)

A. Lorenzetti, *Effects of Good Government in the City*, Siena, Palazzo Pubblico (Mario Appiani - Archivi Alinari)

L. Russolo, *Tina's hair*, private coll. (Luciano Eccher - Alinari Archives)

H. Rousseau, *In the forest*, St.
Petersburg, Hermitage (Alinari Archives)

Giotto, *Joachim's Dream*, Padua,
Scrovegni Chapel
(Mauro Magliani - Alinari Archives)

Turkey sculpture fragments
(Marburg Archives - Alinari Archives)

56

A. Villani,
Il Duce
at the Bologna
airport, 1941
(Alinari Archives -
Villani archives)

A. Villani,
Visit of Fascist
party leaders
to a school, 1940
(Alinari Archives -
Villani archives)

V. Villani,
Baby carriage
factory
in Bologna, 1963
(Alinari Archives -
Villani archives)

V. Villani,
Footwear
machinery
industry, 1974
(Alinari Archives-
Villani archives)

V. Villani, Fashion picture 1960s (Alinari Archives · Villani archives)

V. Villani, 'Lo Spellato', Bologna, Teatro anatomico
(Alinari Archives - Villani archives)

A. Villani, Advertising shot of bathing suits, 1937
(Alinari Archives - Villani archives)

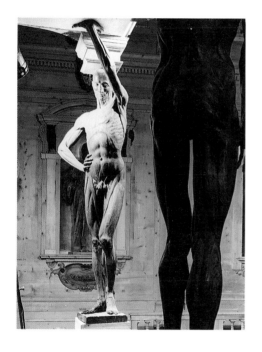

A. Villani, Workmen on the job, 1930s
(Alinari Archives - Villani archives)

V. Villani, Making hemp, 1940s
(Alinari Archives - Villani archives)

V. Villani, Grocery store, 1950s
(Alinari Archives - Villani archives)

V. Villani, A school in the 1940s
(Alinari Archives - Villani archives)

V. Villani, Distillery, 1950s
(Alinari Archives - Villani archives)

V. Villani, Winter landscape, 1940s
(Alinari Archives - Villani archives)

V. Villani, Beniamino Gigli, 1930 (Alinari Archives - Villani archives)

V. Villani, Milva Biolcati, 1960 (Alinari Archives - Villani archives)

V. Villani, Vittorio Gassman, 1960 (Alinari Archives - Villani archives)

V. Villani, Claudio Villa, 1960 (Alinari Archives - Villani archives)

64

The new photographic campaigns

Florence. Galileo.
Machines for numerical control
(Alinari Archives - George Tatge)

In 1986 the Società Alinari once more began photographing on assignment, entrusting the direction and coordination of the new campaigns to George Tatge, who, as occasion demands, is flanked by the most competent professional photographers. The subjects of these campaigns vary in line with the requests: territories, works of art, specific sites, architecture, new restorations, firms, innovative industrial and technological products, industries. ■ **Of** particular importance are the photographic campaign conducted in Pompeii for IBM, the one, currently in progress, commissioned by SEAT Divisione Stet, which provides photographs for the covers of all the Italian telephone directories, as well as others for the Ministry of Arts and Culture, ENI, and for the Army Staff. ■ **S**ome of the new pictures are used in exhibitions and in books; the complete « corpus » in any case ends up in the Archives, enriching and completing the documentation.

Milan, Courtyard in Via Tortona 12 (Alinari Archives · George Tatge)

Tuscan landscapes (Alinari Archives - George Tatge)

The covers of the SEAT
telephone directories

Pistoia, Church of S. Bartolomeo in Pantano, detail of the pulpit
(SEAT Archives - Alinari Archives - George Tatge)

Siena, Sarteano,
Church of S. Niccolò,
A. Di Niccolò,
*Madonna
and Child*,
detail
(SEAT Archives -
Alinari Archives -
George Tatge)

Genoa, S. Maria
di Castello, Loggia
of the Annunciation
(SEAT Archives -
Alinari Archives -
George Tatge)

The Art Printworks

The art printworks

Founded at the end of the 19th century and currently one of the few of its kind still active in the world, the art printworks produce outstanding reproductions, including color, using the old artisan method of collotype (or phototype). ■ **T**he procedure consists of printing a limited number of copies, never more than five hundred, from a crystal plate treated with special inks and continously retouched by the printer. Any prints in excess of this number results in crazing of the plate which can no longer be used. No two prints are exactly alike, for this is not a mass production technique but involves the manual intervention of the artisan. ■ **T**he Alinari Art Printworks (Stamperia d'arte Alinari) thus produce products of the highest quality and particular merit, such as the facsimile reproductions of old photographic or lithographic albums concerning the history of industry, agriculture and landscape, elegant portfolios on specific themes (Leonardo's drawings, the excavations of Pompeii), precious reproductions on silver of famous daguerreotypes such as those by John Ruskin.

Raphael, *Head of an Apostle* (drawing), collotype facsimile

Example of collotype printing

Collotype facsimile of a page in the *Album Semplicini*, Florence 1857
(Museo di Storia della fotografia Fratelli Alinari)

ALBUM DI FOTOGRAFIE

RAPPRESENTANTI GLI ANIMALI PIÙ PREGEVOLI DELL'ESPOSIZIONE AGRARIA TOSCANA

FATTA ALLE RR. CASCINE DI FIRENZE NEL GIUGNO 1857.

Facciata del Palazzo delle RR. Cascine.

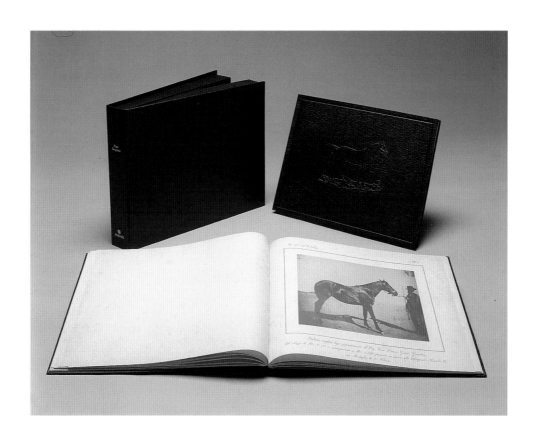

Collotype facsimile from the *Album De Larderel*, Paris circa 1840
(Museo di Storia della fotografia Fratelli Alinari)

**The collotype portfolios:
the great photographs of the past**

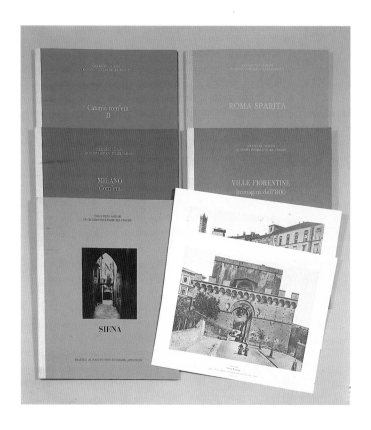

Michelangelo's Drawings in collotype

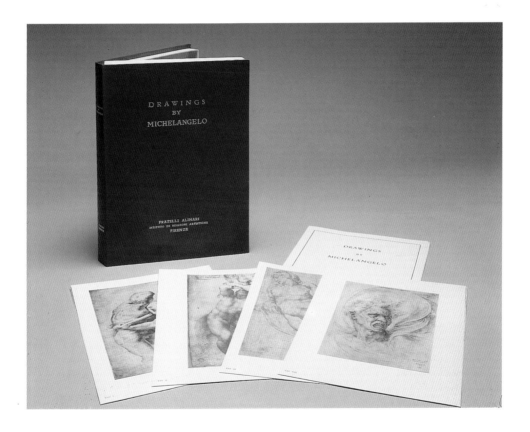

The personalized portfolios

Daguerreotypes, printed with a collotype technique, reproducing Ruskin's original pictures

The Publishing House

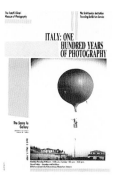

Poster for the exhibition
« Italy one hundred years
of Photography »

Founded in 1885 and then developed by Vittorio Alinari in later years, the publishing house originally brought out art books. As time passed, the range of publications was expanded and at present production keeps pace with the exhibition activities of the Museum, publishing the relative catalogues. ■ **A**part from the exhibition catalogues, Alinari of course also edits other publications on the history and culture of photography, monographs and semiological subjects, all closely linked to the image. ■ **O**f the various series, particular mention goes to the Poster Books, on the principal Italian cities, the collection dedicated to the territory of Tuscany and *Miniatura*, a series issued annually on the history of Italian and

The **Poster-Books** dedicated to the cities

The production of catalogues
of photographic exhibitions

**Poster for the exhibition
« Fernando Pessoa.
Immagini della sua vita »**

European miniatures. The Florentine publishing house also edits « *Fotologia* », the only review in Italy dedicated to studies and research on the history of photography, edited by Italo Zannier and Paolo Costantini. ■ In their elegant, immediately recognizable graphic design, the Alinari publications in the past years have taken a qualitative leap in content as well as form. They are now not only books to look at, but also books to read, where the purely visual aspect is sustained and justified by the text, compiled by well-known authorities. ■ While Alinari publications are available in bookshops, the publishing house also has two bookshops of its own: one connected to the Museum, the other to the exhibition space in Rome.

The series of photographic catalogues
dedicated to Tuscany

The book dedicated
to Verdi made for ENI

The magazine
« Miniatura »
and the
art books

The calendars

The agendas with industrial photographs

The portfolios prepared
for « La Repubblica »

The portfolios and books
made for « Il Giorno »

Brochures and invitations

The Museum

Fratelli Alinari, Florence.
Palazzo Rucellai, det.
(Alinari archives)

The primary and fundamental function of the Museo di Storia della fotografia Fratelli Alinari, inaugurated in 1985 by Sandro Pertini, at the time President of Italy, is that of preserving the 350,000 vintage prints in its safekeeping, including albumen and bromide prints, prints on salt paper, calotypes, daguerreotypes, ambrotypes, stereoscopic prints. ■ The Malandrini, Palazzoli, Gabba, Reteuna and Zannier « collections » have all found their way to the Museum and the greatest 19th and 20th century names include photographers such as Alinari, Anderson, Brogi, Caneva, Nunes Vais, Primoli, Puccini, Ponti, Naya, Wulz, Mollino, Gabinio, Morpurgo, Miniati, Trombetta, Scarabello, Pizzighelli, Peretti Griva, Bara-

V. Paganori, Palazzo Rucellai formerly headquarters of the « Fotografia Romana », late 1800s, albumen print (Museo di Storia della fotografia Fratelli Alinari - Paganori fund)

G.T. Dodero, Street in Genoa, circa 1858,
salt print from a calotype (Museo di Storia
della fotografia Fratelli Alinari - Dodero fund)

N° 1218. Battistero. Firenze

N.M.P. Lerebours, From « Excursions
Daguerriennes »,
Porto di Ripetta in Rome, circa 1841
engraving from a daguerreotype
(Museo di Storia della fotografia
Fratelli Alinari)

valle, Poppi, Tuminello, Unterveger, Antonio and Felice Beato, Balocchi, among
the Italians; Robertson, Fenton, Bourn, Brandt, Zangaki, Sebah among the for-
eigners; and MacPherson, Sommer, Bernoud, Graham, Rive, Flacheron, Von
Gloeden, Van Lint, Noack, among the foreign photographers active in Italy. ■ The
Museum moreover vaunts important collections of cameras, lenses, post cards,
antiques in the field of photography, including an imposing selection of photo
albums, frames, advertising gadgets, both of Italian and foreign make. ■ In 1985
the Museum began a program of exhibitions (on an average of five a year), with
three principal leading themes — history of photography, semiology, monographs
of contemporary photographers under the direction of famous experts. ■ These
exhibitions are held in Palazzo Rucellai and/or installed in other museums in
Italy and abroad. ■ Most of these exhibitions were produced by the Museum

Fratelli Alinari, Portrait of the Corsi Salviati family in their
villa of Sesto, circa 1885, albumen print (Museo di Storia della
fotografia Fratelli Alinari - Alinari fund)

C. Baravalle, Still life, 1925-30,
silver bromide print
(Museo di Storia della fotografia
Fratelli Alinari - Baravalle archives
- *Baravalle donation*)

in collaboration with the Archives, but exhibitions from other countries have also been hosted, thanks to its close contacts with analogous institutions in Italy and abroad, such as Palazzo Fortuny in Venice, the Musée d'Orsay, the Société Française de Photographie and the Bibliothèque Nationale in Paris, the Royal Archives in London, the Corcoran Gallery of Art and the Smithsonian Institution of Washington, the National Geographic, the New York Public Library, the Gulbenkian Foundation in Lisbon. Many of the exhibitions presented in the Museum have subsequently travelled in Italy and abroad, and others still have been specifically planned for other exhibition spaces. ■ **A** permanent auxiliary base for the Museum is the « Spazio Alinari per la fotografia » in Rome, which acts as center for consultation and sales as well as promoting the Alinari exhibitions in the capital.

Garcin and Meylan, Portrait, circa 1841,
daguerreotype (Museo di Storia della
fotografia Fratelli Alinari)

J. B. L. Foucault, Landscape, circa 1845,
daguerreotype (Museo di Storia della
fotografia Fratelli Alinari - *Amici collection*)

Unidentified photographer, Small girl
with dog, circa 1850, daguerreotype
(Museo di Storia della fotografia
Fratelli Alinari)

Unidentified English photographer,
Husband and wife, circa 1850, ambrotype
(Museo di Storia della fotografia Fratelli
Alinari - *Malandrini collection*)

Unidentified photographer, Portrait of the Baudelaire family,
1843, daguerreotype (Museo di Storia della fotografia Fratelli
Alinari - *Galli de' Paratesi collection*)

Unidentified photographer, Marcus Aurelius, Rome, circa 1850, calotype negative
(Museo di Storia della fotografia Fratelli Alinari - *Laurati collection*)

W. Robert Baker,
View over the lake,
circa 1850,
calotype negative
(Museo di Storia
della fotografia
Fratelli Alinari
- Baker fund)

W. Robert Baker,
Country castle
in Great Britain,
circa 1850,
calotype negative
(Museo di Storia
della fotografia
Fratelli Alinari
- Baker fund)

G. Caneva, Rome.
Trinità dei Monti,
circa 1850,
salt print
(Museo di Storia
della fotografia
Fratelli Alinari
- Caneva fund)

P. Poppi,
The Palazzo
Comunale a
Pistoia,
circa 1880,
albumen print
(Museo di Storia
della fotografia
Fratelli Alinari
- Poppi fund)

L. Pesce, Persia Mausoleum of the Sultan Oljeitu, circa 1860, salt print
from a calotype (Museo di Storia della fotografia Fratelli Alinari)

J. Graham,
Pompeii.
Temple of
Mercury,
circa 1852,
albumen
print
from a
calotype
(Museo di
Storia della
fotografia
Fratelli
Alinari
- Graham
fund)

E. Delessert,
Sassari. Rosello
Fountain,
circa 1855,
salt print from a
calotype (Museo
di Storia della
fotografia Fratelli
Alinari)

M. Durand Brager, Kinburn. Ruins of the Fort, circa 1857, salt print from a calotype
(Museo di Storia della fotografia Fratelli Alinari - Durand fund)

F. Beato,
Group of Japanese
dancers,
circa 1860,
albumen print
(Museo di Storia
della fotografia
Fratelli Alinari -
Beato fund -
Malandrini collection)

A. Beato,
Cairo.
The Mameluke
tombs,
circa 1860,
albumen
print
(Museo di Storia
della fotografia
Fratelli Alinari -
Beato fund)

J. Anderson, Roman forum, circa 1860, albumen print
(Museo di Storia della fotografia Fratelli Alinari - Anderson fund)

A. Beato (?), A road in Cairo, circa 1860,
albumen print (Museo di Storia
della fotografia Fratelli Alinari -
Beato fund)

F. Frith, Church of the Holy Sepulchre,
1857, albumen print
(Museo di Storia della fotografia
Fratelli Alinari - Frith fund)

Fratelli Alinari, Pine grove of S. Rossore, circa 1865, albumen print (Museo di Storia della fotografia Fratelli Alinari - Alinari fund)

F. Frith, View
of Jerusalem,
1857, albumen
print
(Museo di
Storia della
fotografia
Fratelli Alinari
- Frith fund)

A. Bernoud,
Panorama
of Florence,
circa 1865,
albumen print
(Museo di Storia
della fotografia
Fratelli Alinari
- Bernoud fund -
*Malandrini
collection*)

G. Sommer, Chairseat weavers, circa 1870, albumen print retouched by hand (Museo di Storia della fotografia Fratelli Alinari - Sommer fund)

C. Ponti, Piazza S. Marco, circa 1870, albumen print (Museo di Storia della fotografia Fratelli Alinari - Ponti fund - *Gabba collection*)

G.B. Unterveger, Trento, circa 1880, albumen print (Museo di Storia della fotografia Fratelli Alinari - Unterveger archives - *Eccher collection*)

Leonor de la Roca,
Manila.
Calle de la Escolta,
circa 1870,
albumen print
(Museo di Storia
della fotografia
Fratelli Alinari
- *Malandrini*
collection)

E. Baldus,
Paris,
Hotel de Ville,
circa 1870,
albumen print
(Museo di Storia
della fotografia
Fratelli Alinari -
Baldus fund
- *Palazzoli*
collection)

T. Cuccioni,
Temple of Sybil
in Tivoli, circa 1870,
albumen print
(Museo di Storia
della fotografia
Fratelli Alinari -
Cuccioni fund)

C. Naya,
Palazzo Pesaro.
Venice, circa 1880,
albumen print
(Museo di Storia
della fotografia
Fratelli Alinari
- Naya fund)

C. e G. Zangaki, Group of Bedouins,
circa 1880, albumen print
(Museo di Storia della fotografia Fratelli
Alinari - Zangaki fund - *Malandrini collection*)

Alguacil f.º - PUENTE DE ALCÁNTARA - TOLEDO

Unidentified photographer, Portrait of A. Lamarmora, circa 1860,
albumen print (Museo di Storia della fotografia
Fratelli Alinari - Pes di Villamarina d'Azeglio family archives)

J. Robertson, Ruins of Severnaia, 1855, salt print from a calotype,
(Museo di Storia della fotografia Fratelli Alinari - Robertson fund - *Palazzoli collection*)

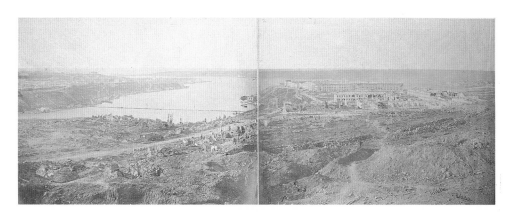

Unidentified photographer, Panorama of the Sciarborasca Road, 1899,
albumen print (Museo di Storia della fotografia Fratelli Alinari - C.A.I. archives Sezione
Ligure - *Malandrini collection*)

Unidentified photographer, Viena. Sculptor in his studio, circa 1880, albumen print (Museo di Storia della fotografia Fratelli Alinari)

M. Schemboche, Antonio Rosselli del Turco and Bice Crespi,
1894, albumen print (Museo di Storia della fotografia Fratelli Alinari -
Schemboche fund - Rosselli del Turco family archives - *Rosselli del Turco donation*)

Schemboche   *Firenze*

Unidentified photographer, Florentine nobles in costume for the Carnival of 1875, albumen print
(Museo di Storia della fotografia Fratelli Alinari - Levi archives)

Unidentified photographer, Prussian nobles, circa 1870, albumen print
(Museo di Storia della fotografia Fratelli Alinari - Pez di Villamarina d'Azeglio family archives)

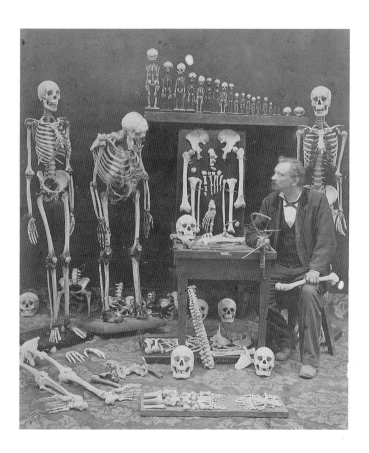

F.P. Michetti, Preparatory studies for
paintings, circa 1885, albumin prints
(Museo di Storia della fotografia
Fratelli Alinari - Michetti fund -
Palazzoli collection)

G. Puccini · F.lli Alinari, Actress, early 1900s (Museo di Storia della fotografia Fratelli Alinari · Puccini archives)

E. Muybridge, « Animal locomotion »,
1887 (Museo di Storia della fotografia
Fratelli Alinari - Muybridge fund -
Palazzoli collection)

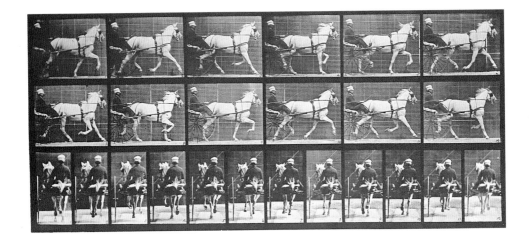

G. Von Gloeden, Child and dog,
1898, albumen print
(Museo di Storia della fotografia
Fratelli Alinari - Von Gloeden fund)

G. Von Gloeden, Family group,
1898, albumen print (Museo di
Storia della fotografia Fratelli Alinari
- Von Gloeden fund)

Louis Amédée Mante e Edmond Goldschmidt, Female nude, 1895-1903, color slide
(Museo di Storia della fotografia Fratelli Alinari - *Ginestra collection*)

Louis Amédée Mante e Edmond Goldschmidt, Female nude,
1895-1903, color slide (Museo di Storia della fotografia
Fratelli Alinari - *Ginestra collection*)

H. Le Lieure, The Geisser brothers, circa 1860, albumen print
retouched by hand (Museo di Storia della fotografia Fratelli
Alinari - Le Lieure fund - Bosio family archives -
Bosio de' Peverelli donation)

C. Pietzner, Adelaide and Sisto di
Borbone Parma, circa 1900 (Museo di
Storia della fotografia Fratelli Alinari
- Borbone Parma archives)

C. Brogi, Portrait of Giuseppe
Pizzighelli, circa 1910, albumen print
(Museo di Storia della fotografia Fratelli
Alinari - Pizzighelli archives - *Pizzighelli donation*)

L. Morpurgo, Calle in Venice, circa 1910, bichromated gum print (Museo di Storia della fotografia Fratelli Alinari - Morpurgo archives - *Morpurgo donation*)

Conrado Perego, Beach of Viareggio, circa 1910, silver bromide print (Museo di Storia della fotografia Fratelli Alinari - Conrado Perego archives - *Malandrini collection*)

Unidentified photographer, Cuzco.
The square and the church, 1950,
(Museo di Storia della fotografia Fratelli
Alinari - *collezione Malandrini*)

E.S. Curtis, A. Klamath. Costume, 1923,
photogravure (Museo di Storia della
fotografia Fratelli Alinari -
Palazzoli collection)

Unidentified photographer, Sculpture by Rodin, circa 1900, celloidine print
(Museo di Storia della fotografia Fratelli Alinari - *Malandrini collection*)

C. Ellis, The dancer Löie Fuller. Paris, 1900, celloidine print
(Museo di Storia della fotografia Fratelli Alinari - *Malandrini collection*)

**R.W. Robinson,
« Suite Springtime »,
circa 1880,
albumen print
(Museo di Storia
della fotografia
Fratelli Alinari
- *Malandrini
collection*)**

**M. Gabinio,
Turin, circa 1920,
silver bromide
print
(Museo di Storia
della fotografia
Fratelli Alinari
- Gabinio fund)**

G. Rey, Dance at the Festival of Mollar Michele (Viù),
1904, celloidine print (Museo di Storia della fotografia
Fratelli Alinari)

L. Betti, Motorcyclist, circa 1930, silver bromide print
(Museo di Storia della fotografia Fratelli Alinari - Betti Borra archives)

C. Scarabello, Self portrait at the easel, 1930-35, silver bromide print
(Museo di Storia della fotografia Fratelli Alinari - Scarabello archives
- *Scarabello donation*)

J. Ortiz-Echagüe, Castillo de Loarre, circa 1930, bromide print
(Museo di Storia della fotografia Fratelli Alinari - *Zannier collection*)

D.R. Peretti Griva, Shepherds, 1931, silver bromide print
(Museo di Storia della fotografia Fratelli Alinari - Peretti Griva fund)

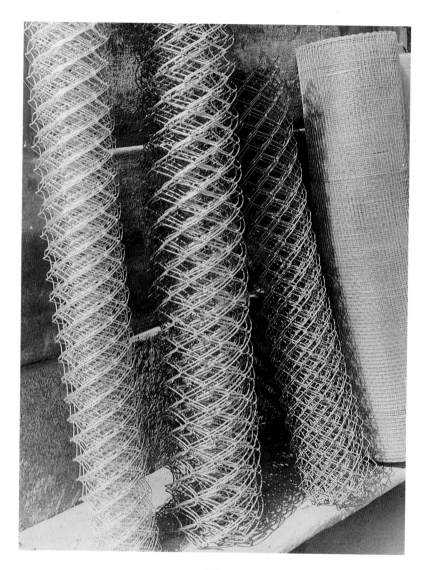

M. Gabinio, Metal nets, 1936, silver bromide print (Museo di Storia della fotografia Fratelli Alinari - Gabinio fund)

Cap. C. Tardivo. Corps of Engineers,
Panorama of Turin, 1906, silver
bromide print, m. 4×0.40 (Museo
di Storia della fotografia Fratelli Alinari
- *Reteuna collection*)

M. Nunes Vais, The sculptor Vincenzo Gemito,
circa 1915, silver bromide print (Museo di Storia
della fotografia Fratelli Alinari - Nunes Vais archives)

M. Castagneri, Self portrait, 1921,
silver bromide print retouched by hand
(Museo di Storia della fotografia
Fratelli Alinari - Castagneri archives)

P. Martina C. Mollino, Turin (aerial stunt), 1942, silver bromide print
(Museo di Storia della fotografia Fratelli Alinari - Mollino fund)

A. Porry-Pastorel, Mussolini arrested
during an interventionist meeting,
1914, silver bromide print
(Museo di Storia della fotografia Fratelli
Alinari - *Zannier collection*)

B. Miniati, Torpedo launched by the
R.T. Aldebaran (Museo di Storia della
fotografia Fratelli Alinari - Miniati
archives - *Miniati donation*)

L. Veronesi, Photogram, 1955, silver bromide print
(Museo di Storia della fotografia Fratelli Alinari - *Zannier collection*)

A. Trombetta, At work, 1910, print on art paper
(Museo di Storia della fotografia Fratelli Alinari · Trombetta archives · *Trombetta donation*)

W. Wulz, Dannunziana, circa 1930, silver bromide print
(Museo di Storia della fotografia Fratelli Alinari - Wulz archives)

C. Wulz, Sphinx, n.d., silver bromide print (Museo di Storia della fotografia Fratelli Alinari - Wulz archives)

G. Vannucci-Zauli, Ballerinas, circa 1946, silver bromide print
(Museo di Storia della fotografia Fratelli Alinari - Vannucci-Zauli archives - *Vannucci-Zauli donation*)

W. Wulz, Wunder-bar, circa 1930, silver bromide print (Museo di Storia della fotografia Fratelli Alinari - Wulz archives)

Unidentified photographer, **Memoir of Archduke Carlo Stefano of Lorena's trip to Greece,** circa 1900, silver bromide print (Museo di Storia della fotografia Fratelli Alinari)

C. Mollino, Untitled, circa 1940, silver bromide print
(Museo di Storia della fotografia Fratelli Alinari - Mollino fund)

V. Balocchi, Study, n.d., silver bromide print (Museo di Storia della fotografia Fratelli Alinari - Balocchi archives)

V. Balocchi, Hands, 1940, silver bromide print (Museo di Storia della fotografia Fratelli Alinari - Balocchi archives)

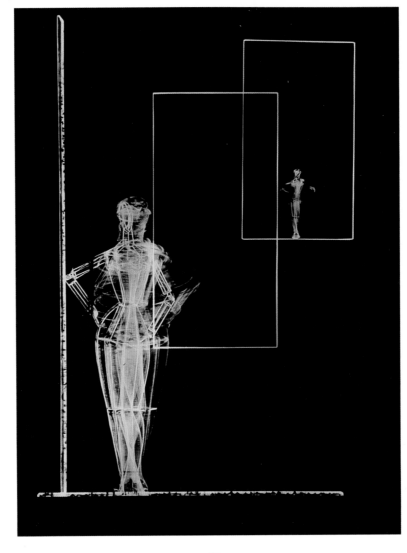

Otto Steinert, **Strenges Ballet**, 1949, silver bromide print (Museo di Storia della fotografia Fratelli Alinari · *Zannier collection*)

L. Freed, Harlem. New York, 1963, silver bromide print (Museo di Storia della fotografia Fratelli Alinari)

M. Giacomelli, I Haven't Hands That
Caress My face, 1962-1963,
bromide print (Museo di Storia
della fotografia Fratelli Alinari -
Giacomelli fund - *Zannier collection*)

C. Colombo, Milan. Via Montenapoleone,
1956, bromide print (Museo di Storia
della fotografia Fratelli Alinari -
Zannier collection)

G. Berengo-Gardin, Venice, circa 1960,
bromide print (Museo di Storia della
fotografia Fratelli Alinari -
Berengo-Gardin fund -
Zannier collection)

P. Monti, Moving flowers, n.d., bromide print
(Museo di Storia della fotografia Fratelli Alinari -
Zannier collection)

P. Gioli, Still life, 1985, cibachrome-stenopeica (Museo di Storia della fotografia Fratelli Alinari - Gioli fund - *Zannier collection*)

G. Sansoni, Portrait of Luigi Veronesi, **SICOF** 1985, cibachrome
(Museo di Storia della fotografia Fratelli Alinari)

F. Bottino, Portrait of Krizia, SICOF 1985, cibachrome (Museo di Storia della fotografia Fratelli Alinari)

Camera Work, 1911, reproduction of the cover
of the famous photography magazine published
in New York by Stieglitz from 1903 to 1917
(Library of the Museo di Storia
della fotografia Fratelli Alinari)

The library

A. Stieglitz, The Steerage, from the
magazine *Camera Work* October 1911,
photogravure (Library of the Museo di
Storia della fotografia Fratelli Alinari)

The extensive library specialized in the history of photography from its origins to modern times is an integral part of the Museum. On the one hand it collects all the Fratelli Alinari publications, and on the other, it constantly adds new works and historical texts to its fund, thanks to exchange programs with the major photographic cultural institutions throughout the world and to an intensive acquisitions policy. ■ **A** useful and indispensable research aid, the library constitutes one of the most important Italian collections dedicated to subjects dealing with photography and is also open to the public for consultation. ■ **T**he multitude of highly interesting publications include monographs on the photographers and

La Fotografia Artistica, Turin,
1904-1916 (Library of the Museo di
Storia della fotografia Fratelli Alinari)

*Bullettino della Società Fotografica
Italiana*, Florence 1889-1912
(Library of the Museo di Storia
della fotografia Fratelli Alinari)

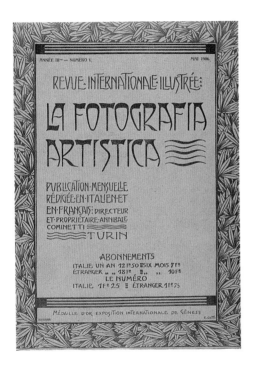

One of the first photography handbooks
published in Italy, 1856 (Library of the
Museo di Storia della fotografia
Fratelli Alinari)

La Camera Oscura, first Italian
photography magazine (Library
of the Museo di Storia della fotografia
Fratelli Alinari)

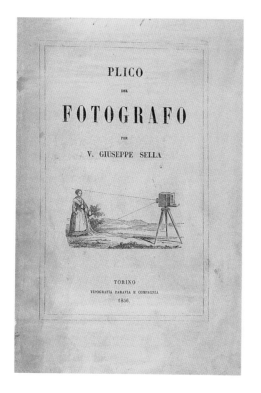

H. Le Lieure, *Turin Ancien et Moderne*,
Turin 1867 (Library of the Museo di
Storia della fotografia Fratelli Alinari)

Photographic dummy for the publication
L'Ensorcelée by J. Barbey d'Aurevilly
with photographs by H. Magron, 1891
(Library of the Museo di Storia della
fotografia Fratelli Alinari)

TURIN

ANCIEN ET MODERNE

H. LE LIEURE, EDITEUR

PHOTOGRAPHIE PARISIENNE – JARDIN PUBLIC, 14 DES REMPARTS

TURIN

COMPTE RENDU

DES SÉANCES

DE L'ACADÉMIE DES SCIENCES.

SÉANCE DU LUNDI 12 AOUT 1839.

PRÉSIDENCE DE M. CHEVREUL.

MÉMOIRES ET COMMUNICATIONS
DES MEMBRES ET DES CORRESPONDANTS DE L'ACADÉMIE.

M. Arago donne communication de la Lettre suivante, qu'il a reçue ce matin de M. le Ministre de l'Intérieur.

« Monsieur et cher collègue, la loi qui accorde une récompense nationale à M. Daguerre ayant reçu la sanction du Roi, il ne reste à publier sa découverte. J'ai pensé que le moyen le meilleur et le plus convenable était de la communiquer à l'Académie des Sciences. Je vous prie de me faire savoir si elle pourra recevoir cette communication dans la séance de lundi prochain, à laquelle pourront être invités MM. les Membres de l'Académie des Beaux-Arts.

« Agréez, Monsieur et cher collègue, etc. »

L'Académie accepte avec empressement l'offre de M. le Ministre. La communication des procédés de MM. Niépce et Daguerre aura lieu dans la séance ordinaire de lundi prochain.

Acts of the Paris Academy of Sciences, contribution of Arago of August 12, 1839, in which he announces Daguerre's invention (Library of the Museo di Storia della fotografia Fratelli Alinari)

their work, treatises and historic manuals, catalogues. The principal historical and contemporary photographic magazines are the subject of particular attention including the complete series of the *Bollettino della Società Fotografica Italiana*, which was first published in Florence in 1889, and the prestigious *Fotografia Artistica*, published in Turin from 1904 to 1916, two of the best-known Italian journals. A real rarity, one of the few complete sets in the world and the only one in Italy that can be consulted, consists of all the issues of the magazine *Camera Work*, directed by Stieglitz and published in New York from 1903 to 1917.

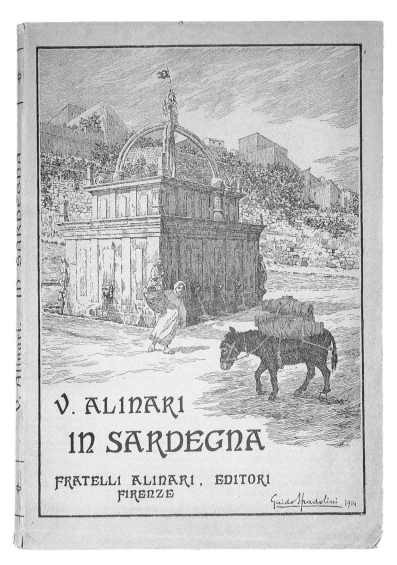

V. ALINARI

IN SARDEGNA

FRATELLI ALINARI, EDITORI
FIRENZE

Guido Spadolini 1914

Paesaggi italici nella Divina Commedia,
September 1921, the last publication
edited by Vittorio Alinari (Library of
the Museo di Storia della fotografia
Fratelli Alinari)

Fratelli Alinari Editori, 1909
(Library of the Museo di Storia
della fotografia Fratelli Alinari)

Le ceramiche d'Italia, publication of
Fratelli Alinari Soc. An. I.D.E.A. circa
1925 (Library of the Museo di Storia
della fotografia Fratelli Alinari)

Megaletoscope: apparatus for observing enlarged photographs,
constructed by Carlo Ponti, Venice 1862
(Museo di Storia della fotografia Fratelli Alinari - *Ginestra donation*)

Photographic equipment

Fotocamera for chromatic selections
6×9, 1930-1935 (Museo di Storia della
fotografia Fratelli Alinari)

At present over 1000 cameras, lenses and instruments related to the history of photography are housed in the Museum and constitute an important sector of the collections. ■ **T**he original fund of old equipment once used by the Alinaris, unique and important documents of the extraordinary technical skill achieved and unceasingly pursued in over a century of commitment to photographic studies, has been increased throughout the years by a variety of other cameras and studio equipment. The sector dedicated to the technical aspects of photography owes much to the sensibility of various donors and scholars. ■ **T**he contribution this sector makes to the history of photography is fundamental, for it documents the evolution of the photograph from the point of view of technology

Enlargement apparatus for negatives
9 x 12 and for projection, I.C.A. Dresda
(Museo di Storia della fotografia Fratelli Alinari)

Reproduction apparatus, autotype and trichrome, circa 1915.
(Museo di Storia della fotografia Fratelli Alinari)

Collodium camera, circa 1860
(Museo di Storia della
fotografia Fratelli Alinari)

and not only in the aesthetic sense. The whole history of the technical means involved in the development of photography from its pioneer days to mass diffusion is presented: from the camera oscura equipped with lenses made by the well-known French firm of Lerebours for daguerrotypes, to the large wooden bellows cameras for collodion plates, studio models and for use outdoors, and the three precious metaletoscopes and the stereo cameras. The revolution begun in 1888 by the first Kodak box camera that used a roll of film marks the beginning of amateur photography as a popular pastime, opening the way to portable hand cameras, many of which became part of the history of photography and are now in the Museum collections.

Stereoscopic camera Stereo Photo
Binocle by C.P. Goerz, Berlin 1899
(Museo di Storia della fotografia Fratelli
Alinari - *Malandrini collection*)

« Jumelle Sigriste » camera 6.5×9,
Paris 1898 (Museo di Storia della
fotografia Fratelli Alinari)

Art-Deco Rolleicord camera 6×6,
1933-1936 (Museo di Storia della
fotografia Fratelli Alinari)

Steinheil spectrograph, circa 1890
(Museo di Storia della fotografia
Fratelli Alinari)

Lamperti and Garbagnati travelling
camera, Milan 1890-1900 (Museo di
Storia della fotografia Fratelli Alinari)

Telefoto lenses for large format
photography, circa 1870-80 (Museo di
Storia della fotografia Fratelli Alinari)

Brass frame, circa 1920 (Museo di Storia
della fotografia Fratelli Alinari -
Batacchi collection)

The picture presented and the picture preserved

Advertising photo and frame for
Fratelli Alinari, 1905 (Museo di Storia
della fotografia Fratelli Alinari)

The multitude of ways in which the photographic image has been presented and preserved is an inseparable part of the history of photography and the profound social and aesthetic revolution it determined. ■ The relationship between the picture and the context in which it is presented to the viewer, in the more intimate ambient of the family album or in the regal preciousness of a carved frame or a richly decorated silver and enamel case, represents a chapter in the history of photography still in need of further study but unquestionably of great interest. ■ A collection consisting of several hundred frames for photographs is there-

**'Souvenir' album bound in leather
with decorations in gold**

fore quite at home in the Museum. Examples range from traditional wooden frames of the type used for paintings, to more complex models with allegorical references to the photographic subject matter, mirrors for example, up to others dating to the early 1900s where the faces of the time are enclosed in the sinuous lines of Art Nouveau designs. ■ In like manner, the extraordinary collection of albums in the Museum bears witness to the prestige and value that was eventually attributed to the photograph. The enamels, silver, ivory and prized woods used, as well as the most precious fabrics, enrich and indirectly confer a new dignity to the photos carefully preserved inside these albums.

Album for carte-de-visite photographs with
binding in leather and mother-of-pearl, circa 1890
(Museo di Storia della fotografia
Fratelli Alinari)

Rome, « Spazio Alinari per la
fotografia »: « Donna. "La Belle Epoque"
nella sala di posa Alinari », det.

Photographic exhibitions

« Immagini del Chianti », det.

Alinari devotes particular attention to photographic exhibitions. ■ **O**riginal exhibitions, complete with catalogue-books, multi-media and other communication-related aids, centered on the history, traditions, economy, the cultural, social and artistic development of the regions of Italy, have been organized, capitalizing on this unique patrimony of photographs and the support of a highly prestigious scientific and technical committee, aided and abetted as required by outstanding critics and historians in the various fields and semiologies. Exhibitions dedicated to the most important 20th-century Italian and foreign photographers have also been realized. ■ **I**n recent years over 35 exhibitions have been presented in the Museo di Storia della fotografia Fratelli Alinari in Palazzo Rucellai and another 45 installed elsewhere, including travelling shows, in over 80 cities in Italy and abroad, centered on three main themes: history of photography, se-

Florence,
Museo Alinari:
« Luci e Ombre »
(above) and
« Immagini del
Casentino »

« Bonnard photographe », det.

« Crown and Camera », det.

« Fernando Pessoa », det.

209

« Immagini del Casentino », det.

miology, monographs on contemporary photographers. ■ In achieving results of the highest quality, Alinari follows tried and tested criteria in each phase of the realization of the project. ■ A team of researchers does all the historical research, indispensable in procuring the iconographic and photographic material, availing itself of the Alinari Archives, and of whatever the public and private institutions in the territory involved have to offer, in museums and collections all over the world. ■ The aims of the photographic campaigns expressly conducted by Alinari photographers is to document the historical, economic, social and artistic situation of today, as well as to revisit the sites that research turns up in the Archive photos, in order to compare the past with the present. ■ The photographic image, in its aesthetics and as a means of communication, in a scenographic-photographic context consisting of skillfull enlargements, suitable lighting, intelligent itineraries to guide the visitor, is transformed into a spectacle that can be enjoyed as a true work of art. ■ The Museo Alinari has also hosted exhibitions from other internationally known institutions, collaborating closely with, for instance, the Fox Talbot Museum in England, the Gulbenkian Foundation

Florence, Palazzo Vecchio: « Alle origini
della fotografia: un itinerario toscano.
1839/1880 »

Milan, Arengario: « Milano, le 20 città »

« Donna "La Belle Epoque" nella
sala di posa Alinari », det.

in Lisbon, Windsor Castle, the New York Public Library, the Bibliothèque Nationale in Paris and the Corcoran Gallery in Washington, Magnum Agency, the National Geographic Magazine, the Musée d'Orsay, etc. ■ **O**ther exhibitions were planned and installed by Alinari for Public corporations in cities of Piedmont, Lombardy, the Alto Adige, the Veneto, Friuli Venezia-Giulia, Emilia-Romagna, the Marches and Tuscany, Lazio, Sicily. Some of them have circulated abroad, including the exhibition « Das Italien der Alinari » organized in Frankfurt. « Italy: One Hundred Years of Photography » is travelling through more than 25 of the largest cities in North America, thanks to the collaboration of the Smithsonian Institution in Washington. The exhibition « The Italian Americans », installed in Ellis Island in New York as part of the Columbus celebrations, will visit various cities in the United States, while the exhibition « Immagini delle Marche negli Archivi Alinari, 1880-1940 » will travel to four cities in Argentina. ■ **A**ll this is thanks to the determining participation of those who have always believed in photography as an invaluable and indispensable witness to our culture and our traditions.

Rome, San Michele: « Roma e il Lazio negli Archivi Alinari »

Bologna,
Civico Museo
Archeologico:
« Odyssey.
L'arte della
fotografia
al National
Geographic »

Rome,
« Spazio Alinari
per la
fotografia »:
« Donna
"La Belle Epoque"
nella sala
di posa Alinari »

**Trieste,
Galleria del
Tergesteo:
« La Trieste
dei Wulz »**

**« La Trieste
dei Wulz »,
det.**

**« Crown
and Camera »,
det.**

Florence, Museo Alinari: « Edward Weston »

Frankfurt, Kunstverein: « Das Italien der Alinari »

Washington, The IMF Visitors Center:
« Italy: one hundred years of photography »

Turin, Lingotto: « La Fabbrica di immagini »